BE THOU MY VISION

Creative Settings for the Pianist in Worship

Arranged by Marilynn Ham

ADVANCED

Lillenas PUBLISHING COMPANY
KANSAS CITY, MO 64141

CONTENTS

Be Thou My Vision

Traditional
Arranged by Marilynn Ham

Slowly, with freedom ♩ = ca. 80

Gently, a little faster ♩ = ca. 86

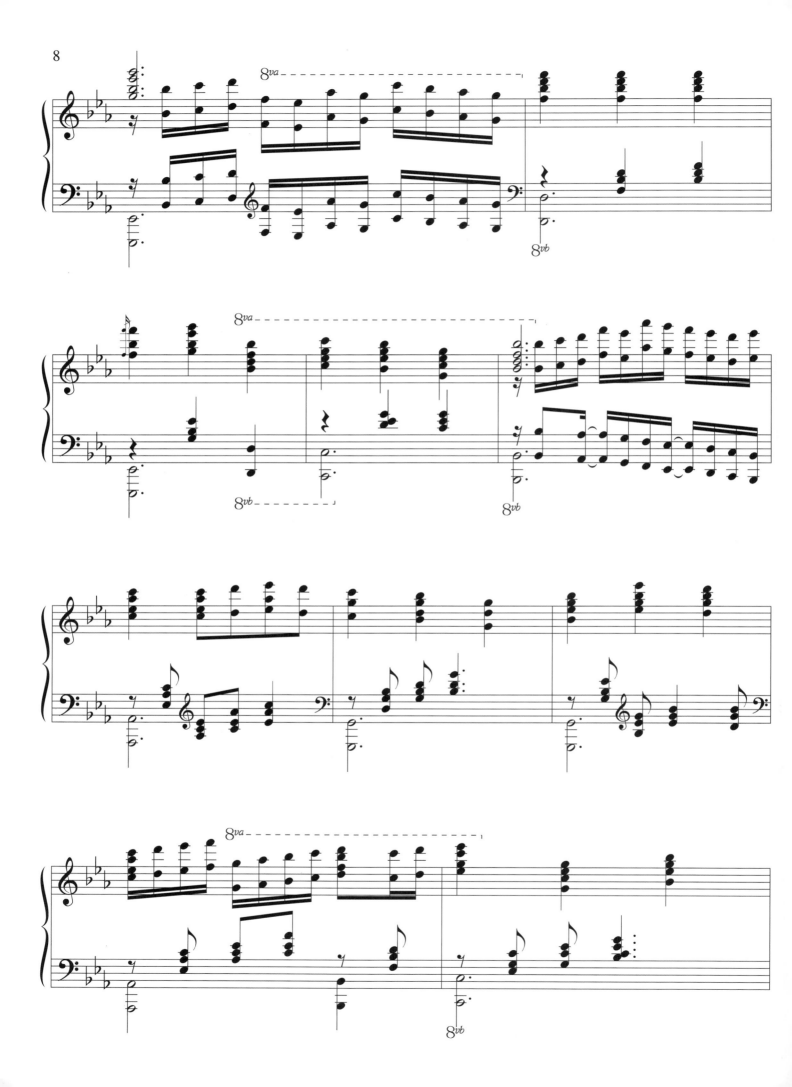

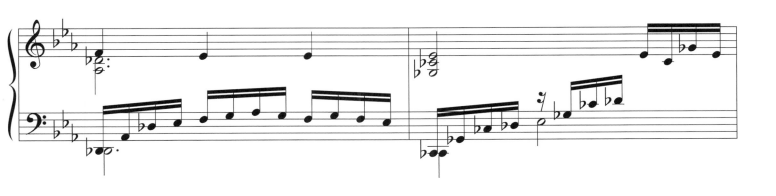

2-12-2023

All That Thrills My Soul

THORO HARRIS
Arranged by Marilynn Ham

Joyful, Joyful We Adore Thee

LUDWIG VAN BEETHOVEN
Arranged by Marilynn Ham

As the Deer

MARTIN NYSTROM
Arranged by Marilynn Ham

Delicately, a little slower

My Faith Has Found a Resting Place

Traditional
Arranged by Marilynn Ham

Expressive and legato ♩ = ca.76

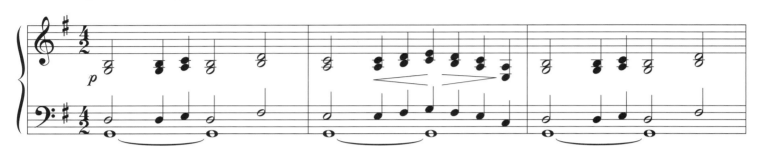

una corda

Simply and steadily

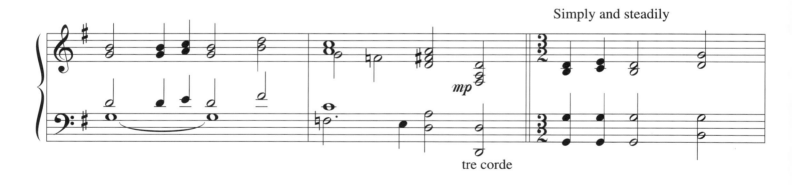

tre corde

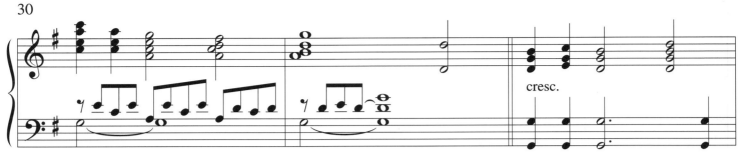

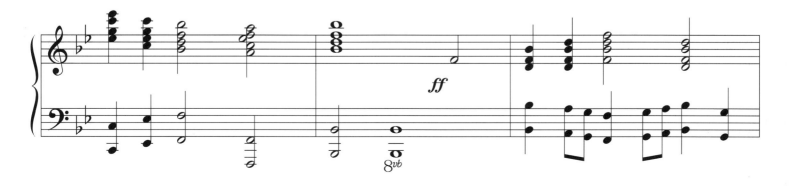

It Is Finished

with
Because He Lives

WILLIAM J. GAITHER
Arranged by Marilynn Ham

*"Because He Lives"

With excitement

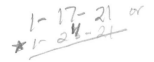

Trusting Jesus Medley

Trust and Obey
'Tis So Sweet to Trust in Jesus

Arranged by Marilynn Ham

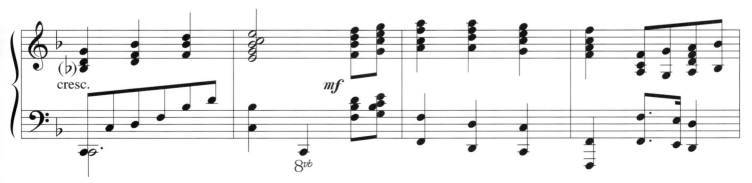

Rubato

*"'Tis So Sweet to Trust in Jesus"

Gently with expression

No One Ever Cared for Me like Jesus

CHARLES F. WEIGLE
Arranged by Marilynn Ham

Tenderly, with expression ♩ = ca. 63

5-16-2021
2-12-2023

To God Be the Glory

WILLIAM H. DOANE
Arranged by Marilynn Ham

Spirited ♩ = ca. 112

Lightly

Majestic, broader tempo

A little faster

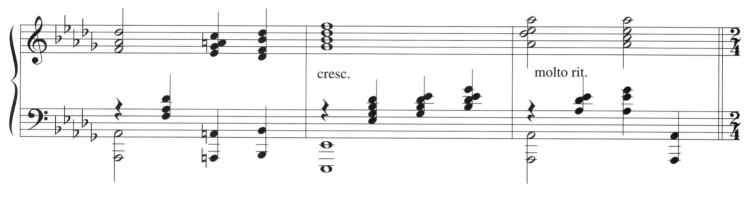

Battle Hymn of the Republic

Traditional American Melody
Arranged by Marilynn Ham